SHREDDING PAGANINI

HEAVY METAL GUITAR MEETS 9 MASTERPIECES BY NICCOLÒ PAGANINI

GERMAN SCHAUSS

CD recorded by German Schauss

Guitar on cover courtesy Schecter Guitar Research

Baroque ornament: © iStockphoto.com / Scott Krycia

Alfred Music
P.O. Box 10003
Van Nuys, CA 91410-0003
alfred.com

ISBN-10: 0-7390-8037-7 (Book & CD)
ISBN-13: 978-0-7390-8037-5 (Book & CD)

ISBN-10: 0-7390-9560-9 (Book & CD & DVD)
ISBN-13: 978-0-7390-9560-7 (Book & CD & DVD)

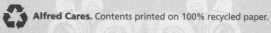
Alfred Cares. Contents printed on 100% recycled paper.

CONTENTS

A compact disc is available with this book. Using the disc will help make learning more enjoyable and the information more meaningful. Listening to the CD will help you correctly interpret the rhythms and feel of each example. The symbol to the left appears next to each song or example that is performed on the CD. The track number below each symbol corresponds directly to the example you want to hear. Track 1 will help you tune to this CD.

ABOUT THE AUTHOR

German Schauss is a guitarist, composer, author, and educator who teaches at Berklee College of Music and other music schools. He performs and tours as the leader of his own band and with other internationally known artists. German writes music for commercials, TV, and video games, and has been named one of the 50 fastest guitarists of all time by *Guitar World* magazine. He is signed to Steve Vai's Digital Nations label. The author of *Shredding Bach* (Alfred/NGW #34922) and *The Total Shred Guitarist* (Alfred/NGW #36573), German also writes the popular monthly column "Instant Shredding" for Germany's biggest guitar magazine, *Gitarre & Bass*.

PHOTO BY JI YEON SONG

German uses and proudly endorses: Ernie Ball/Music Man, Bogner, Rocktron, PreSonus, Native Instruments, Maxon, Guyatone, Morley, Dunlop, Voodoo Labs, Pigtronix Pedals, DiMarzio, Zoom, Tremol-No, D'Addario, Planet Waves, MakeMusic, and Pedaltrain products.

For more about German Schauss and his music, please visit:
www.germanschauss.com

Acknowledgements

I would like to thank my wife Ji Yeon for her never-ending patience, guidance, and love. Furthermore, I would like to thank my family for their love and belief in me and my music. I would also like to thank Jon Finn and Koji Tsumoto for reminding me to stay true to my artistic vision and to simply enjoy playing the best instrument on the planet: the guitar. Thanks to all of my friends and fans around the world for their support, positive thoughts, and love—you are all an inspiration to me! Additionally, thanks to Burgess Speed and the teams at Workshop Arts and Alfred Music Publishing.

INTRODUCTION

Niccolò Paganini was, undoubtedly, one of the greatest virtuosos that ever lived. His skills on the violin were above and beyond anything that had been known before him, and his playing style and inventive techniques had a great impact on the technical advancement of the instrument.

Paganini was born in Genoa, Italy on October 27, 1782 and received musical training from a young age. His skills and technical prowess led him to many teachers who either declined to instruct him, because he was too advanced, or directed him to their own teachers to further his studies. After a disappointing search for a mentor, Paganini decided to train himself, leading him to practice up to 15 hours a day to perfect his skill.

He toured Europe from the late 1790s to the 1830s and also had short engagements as musical director or conductor at various royal houses in Europe. Although he was a gifted composer and guitar player, many critics stated that his compositional work was too *homophonic* (having a single melody line with chordal accompaniment) and was lacking the necessary counterpoint. While this may or may not have been true, ultimately, the music was written to showcase the solo violin, which it did beyond anything that had been composed up to that point.

Paganini's lifestyle was similar to that of a modern rock star. His excesses led to declining health at a young age, greatly interfering with his performances and musical work and incapacitating him for weeks, or even months. He also tried his hand at business, opening a casino in Paris that soon went bankrupt and left him in financial ruins. He spent the remainder of his days in Marseilles and Nice, France where he died on May 27, 1840.

Paganini's life was a succession of triumphs and failures and his amazing playing skills led the public to believe he was in a pact with the devil, especially since he refused the sacrament of Last Rites twice and was denied a proper Christian burial until many years after his death.

About This Book

Shredding Paganini is for intermediate to advanced guitarists who can read standard music notation or TAB and have a firm grasp on basic guitar technique and music theory (scale theory, diatonic harmony, etc.). However, you do not already have to be a "shred" guitarist to benefit from this book. As you learn each new piece, you will also be introduced to the shred techniques required to play it.

For this book, I have collected and arranged nine pieces that are very different in style and approach. They range from simple studies to the most advanced and demanding compositions. Try to pace yourself and break the pieces down into sections. You may even dissect challenging passages for your own technical or compositional study. Paganini was a master at developing theme and variations and combining these ideas with the most difficult playing techniques. Some of his humanly "impossible" phrases and sections were possible to *him* because he suffered from a physical genetic condition that led to extreme joint flexibility.

As always, try to absorb, understand, and apply what you learn to your own thinking and playing. We are all different, and there are always ways to work on and develop our own voice, especially when learning from a master like Paganini.

I hope you enjoy the pieces in this book, and that they help you grow as a musician.

Niccolò Paganini (1782–1840).

ANDANTINO VARIATO

Brief Musical Analysis

Paganini was not only one of the greatest violinists of all time, he was also an accomplished guitarist who composed several pieces for solo guitar, as well as guitar accompanied by other string instruments.

A great introduction to his virtuoso work is the *Grand Sonata in A Major* for solo guitar. We will look at the first variation of "Andantino Variato," which is the third movement of the *Grand Sonata.*

The piece begins with two pickup notes leading into the first full measure. The basic *motif* of this variation (a motif is a short, recurring melodic or rhythmic figure) consists of two ascending *triads* (three-note chords) followed by a fast descending scale run. The measure to the right shows the basic idea behind this variation.

Measures 1–2

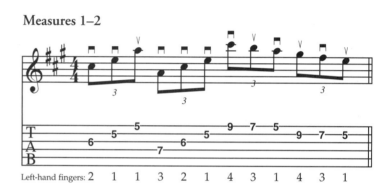

The technical challenge to playing this theme is the combination of *sweep picking* (on the triads) and *alternate picking* (on the scale runs). Sweep picking is a technique that utilizes the picking direction, either ascending or descending, to play notes that are located on adjacent strings in one "sweeping" motion. This technique is used mostly when playing arpeggios. Alternate picking consists of changing your picking direction (⊓ ∨ ⊓ ∨ etc.) with each new note.

The idea is repeated in the next two measures outlining an E7 chord, an A Major chord, and an E Major chord. When playing these sections, strive for an even sound and only lightly mute the strings to avoid any unnecessary noise or ringing notes.

⊓ = Downstroke

∨ = Upstroke

The motif is picked up again in measures 5 and 6 (which are exactly the same as measures 1 and 2) but then leads into an A Major and an E Major arpeggio. Both of these arpeggios are performed with sweep picking.

Measure 7

Following is the first half of the first variation of "Andantino Variato." This piece, with its combination of alternate and sweep picking, is an excellent "warm-up." It also gives you insight into Paganini's thinking and compositional ideas. After playing the example below, I challenge you to continue arranging the second half of this variation and to learn more about his solo guitar music. (Note: the tempo indication at the beginning of the piece, ♩ = 140, indicates the music is to be played at a rate of 140 quarter-note beats per minute, or *bpm*.)

You can hear the arrangement of this piece on Track 2. Track 3 is the backing track (minus the solo guitar) at the intended tempo, and Track 4 is the backing track at a slower tempo.

ANDANTINO VARIATO

Backing Tracks
3—Fast
4—Slow

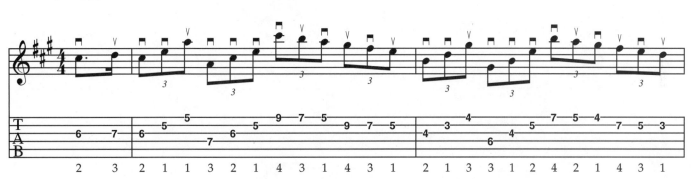

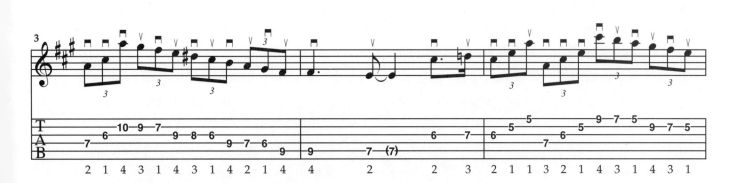

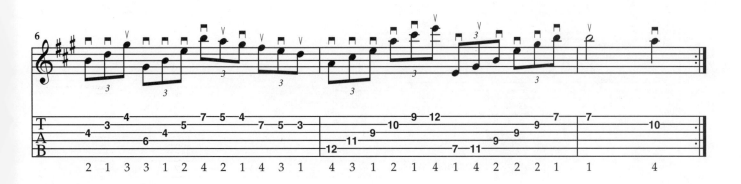

ROMANCE FOR SOLO GUITAR

Brief Musical Analysis

Paganini's "Romance for Solo Guitar" is a great example of the expressive, more sensitive side of this ferocious virtuoso! This piece is in the key of A Minor and the meter is $\frac{6}{8}$, which gives it a very light and almost dance-like quality. In $\frac{6}{8}$ time, there are six beats per measure, with the eighth note receiving the beat. This meter should be counted: 1-&-ah, 2-&-ah, etc.

For example:

Count: 1   &   ah   2   &   ah

The harmonic structure of this piece is quite simple, covering rudimentary chord progressions such as i to V7 (Amin to E7) or iv to i (Dmin to Amin). In measures 7–8, there is a short *tonicization* of the V chord (Esus and E7). This is accomplished through the use of a *secondary dominant,* or a dominant chord built on the 5th degree above any chord other than the *tonic* (first chord of the scale or key). In the case below, the secondary dominant B7 creates greater pull towards, and temporarily tonicizes, the Esus and E7 chords.

Measures 7–8

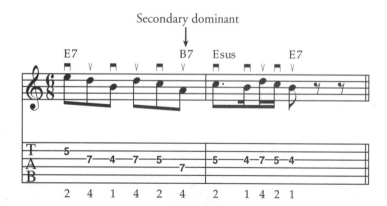

The piece ends with an "improvised" *cadenza* leading back to the i chord, A Minor. A cadenza is an improvised solo at the beginning of a piece, or, more commonly, at the end before the last chord.

The cadenza in this piece is based on a G♯ Diminished 7th sweep arpeggio. A *diminished 7th* arpeggio, composed entirely of minor 3rds (1–♭3–♭5–♭♭7, etc.), is a symmetrical structure that can be repeated in increments of minor 3rds up or down the neck. In other words, you can play the following example starting three frets higher than written, then three frets higher—or three frets lower, then three frets lower, etc.

Play the example below, and then try moving it up or down the fretboard in three-fret increments. You will find that it has the same diminished sound in every location.

Measure 16

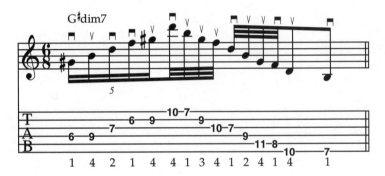

On the next page is an arrangement of the "Romance for Solo Guitar" theme. You can listen to this piece on Track 5. Track 6 is the backing track at the original tempo, and Track 7 is the backing track at a slower tempo.

ROMANCE FOR SOLO GUITAR

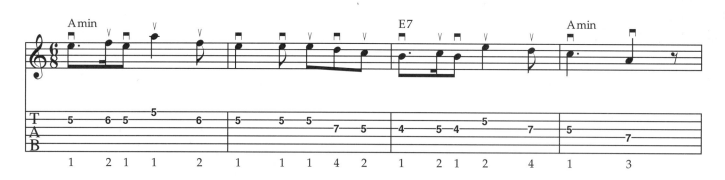

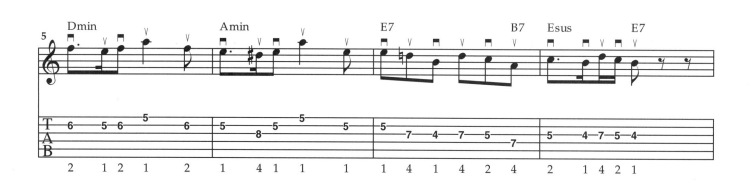

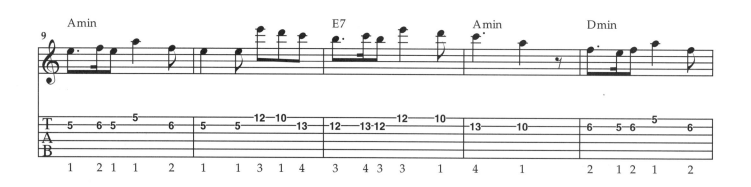

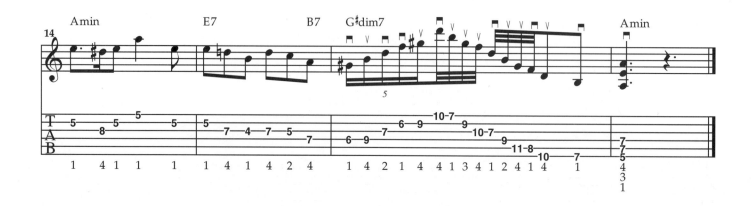

CONCERTO NO. 4 IN D MINOR

Brief Musical Analysis

Among Paganini's numerous compositions are many works for full orchestra and solo violin, including "Concerto No. 4 in D Minor." In this chapter, we will be learning an arrangement of this composition's opening theme.

The main theme begins with a pickup measure that leads into a descending scale idea. The pickup notes become very powerful when the whole orchestra joins in on the first full measure. Check out the excerpt below.

Measures 1–4

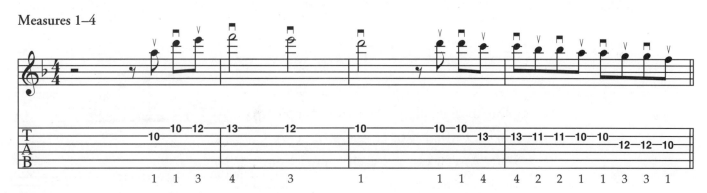

The motif above is repeated and played in different variations, with either ascending or descending scale ideas and various harmonic tools like secondary dominants (see page 8).

The second theme is more subtle and of a calmer nature. Try to play the notes expressively, adding *vibrato* and even sliding into notes when it seems effective. Vibrato is a series of quick, tiny bends that creates a kind of warbling sound. The sliding technique, also known as *glissando*, is accomplished by playing a note, then, while maintaining pressure on the fretboard, sliding up or down to another note on the same string. Now, check out an excerpt from the second theme below.

Measures 10

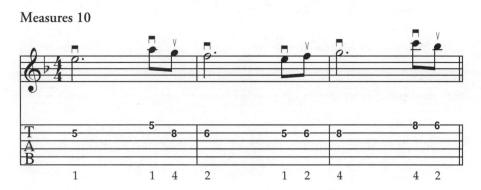

In this piece, Paganini's compositional approach is very symmetrical, introducing five motifs that are all eight bars in length and repeat throughout the entire concerto in different variations.

Paganini also makes effective use of *approach tones*. An approach tone is a *non-diatonic* note that precedes another note from a half step above or below. (Non-diatonic means that it doesn't belong to the scale.) The example below shows the approach tone F♯ leading to G. Note that this tone is outside of the scale being used, D Harmonic Minor, which consists of the notes D–E–F–G–A–B♭–C♯ (scale tones: 1–2–♭3–4–5–♭6–7).

Measures 37–38

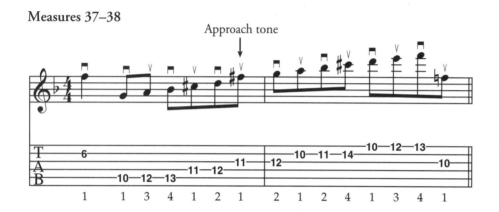

The example to the right illustrates the use of approach tones within a D Minor 7th arpeggio (D–F–A–C, or 1–♭3–5–♭7). As you can see, each approach tone is placed on a weak part of the beat and leads into a chord tone.

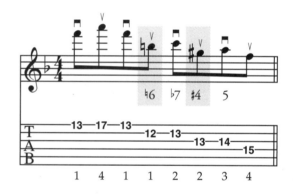

Watch out for the *trill* in measures 13 and 16 (see measure 16 to the right). A trill, indicated by the symbol *tr*〰, is a rapid series of hammer-ons and pull-offs between two notes, in this case G♯ and A.

Measure 16

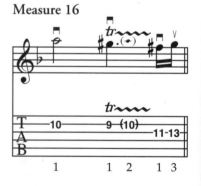

The theme to "Concerto No. 4 in D Minor" is relatively simple, but it is very powerful and a lot of fun to play. If you are interested, get the recording of the entire concerto, and the score as well, and try to study and possibly arrange more of this great piece.

Track 8 demonstrates the full arrangement, and Tracks 9 and 10 are fast and slow backing tracks for you to practice with.

Concerto No. 4 in D Minor

Backing Tracks
9—Fast
10—Slow

H = Hammer-on

P = Pull-off

♩ = 120

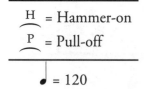

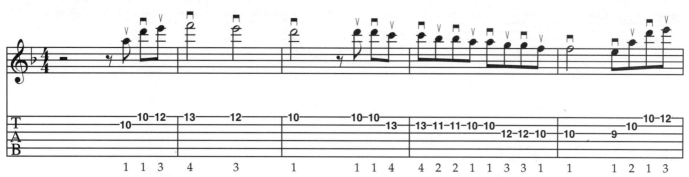

Ottava alta. Play one octave higher than written.

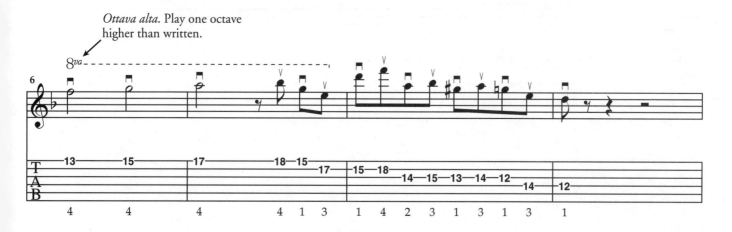

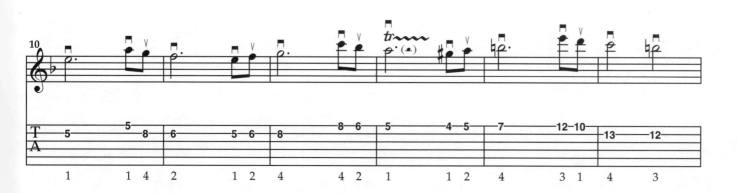

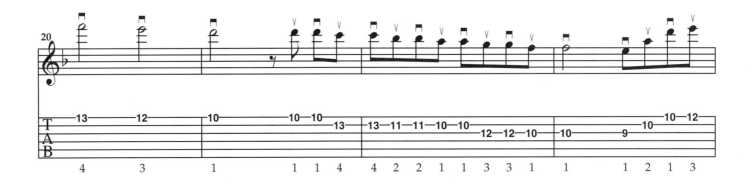

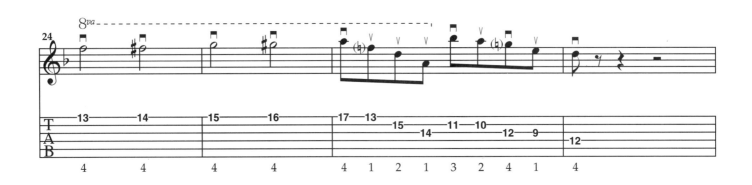

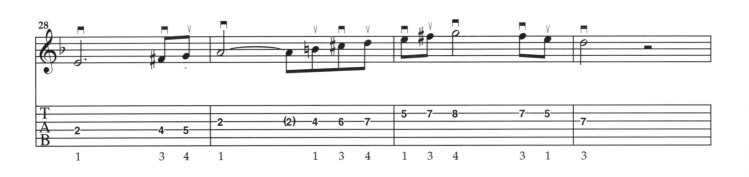

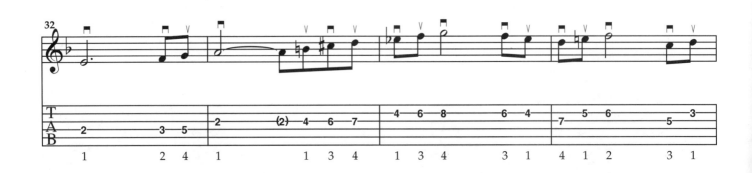

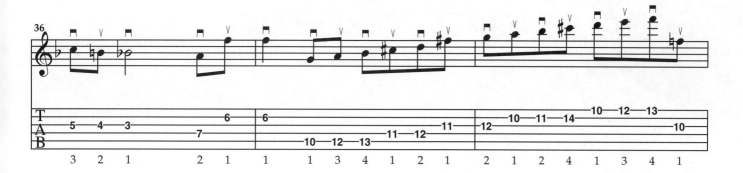

Grace note. A small note played quickly,
as an embellishment, before the main note.

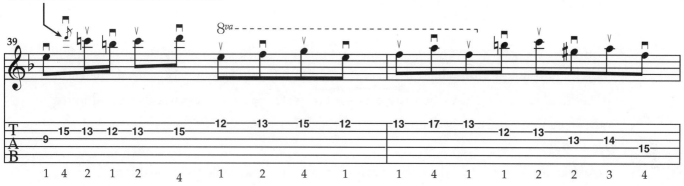

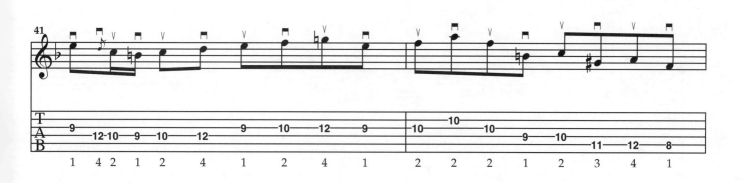

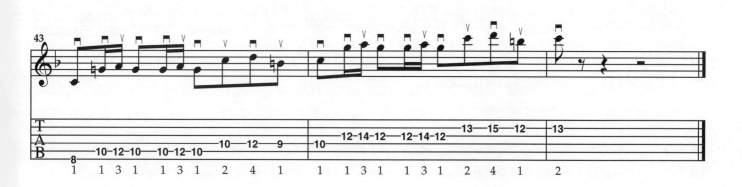

MOTO PERPETUO

Brief Musical Analysis

Paganini's "Moto Perpetuo," also known as "Perpetual Motion," is an excellent chops-builder for alternate picking. The continuous melodic lines—played at a fast, steady tempo—are great for building speed and stamina in a very musical context.

This book features an arrangement of the composition up to the first repeat. For study and practice purposes, try breaking the music down into different sections. In general, the entire piece should be played with alternate picking, but there are a few measures that could utilize other techniques, such as sweeping or *slurring* (hammer-ons, pull-offs, or slides).

Let's take a look at the first three measures and analyze the harmonic content. (Note: The first, incomplete measure—measure 0—is a pickup that starts on beat 3.) The *scalar*, or scale-based, lines in "Moto Perpetuo" reflect chords, melody, and harmony all at the same time. You can analyze the harmony by beat, or just by measure—whichever is easier for you.

Measures 0–3

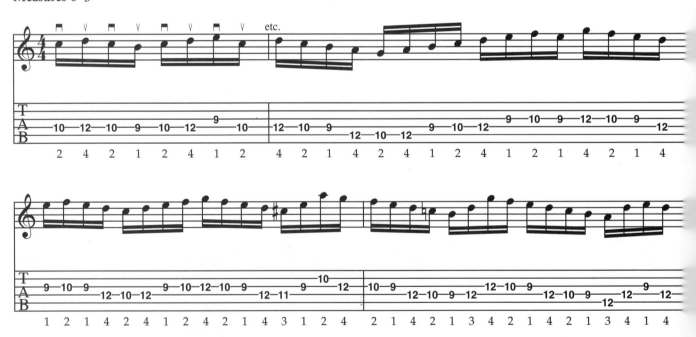

If you look at the first and third notes of each beat, or sixteenth-note grouping, you can discern the harmony very clearly. In the pickup measure, these notes are C and E, which produces the overall tonality of a C Major chord (C–E–G). The next measure suggests a G7 chord (G–B–D–F), which leads back to C Major in the second measure. The third measure includes two chords: G7 on beats 1 and 2, and A Minor (A–C–E) on beats 3 and 4.

Not all of the lines in this piece are scalar—some are based on arpeggios, as in the example below.

Measure 24 arpeggiates a D Major chord on beats 1 and 3, and an A7 on beats 2 and 4. Practice this phrase slowly, and pay close attention to the fingering and alternate picking patterns.

Measure 24

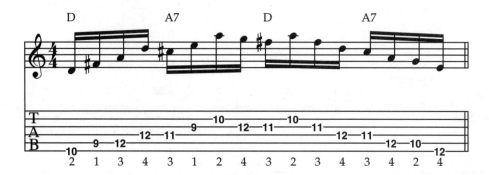

Paganini also utilizes patterns of ascending and descending 3rds, as in measures 30 and 31.

Measures 30–31

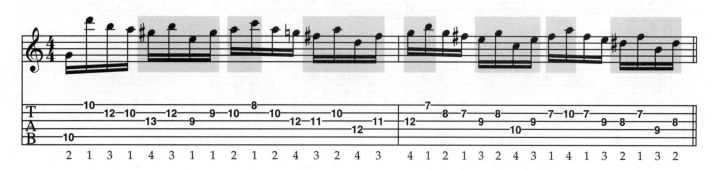

"Moto Perpetuo" covers a lot of harmonic ground. It starts out in the key of C Major and utilizes secondary dominants (see page 8) to target other chords within the key, as well as the A Melodic Minor scale and its chords.

You can hear the arrangement of "Moto Perpetuo" on Track 11. Track 12 is the backing track at the intended tempo, and Track 13 is the backing track at a slower tempo.

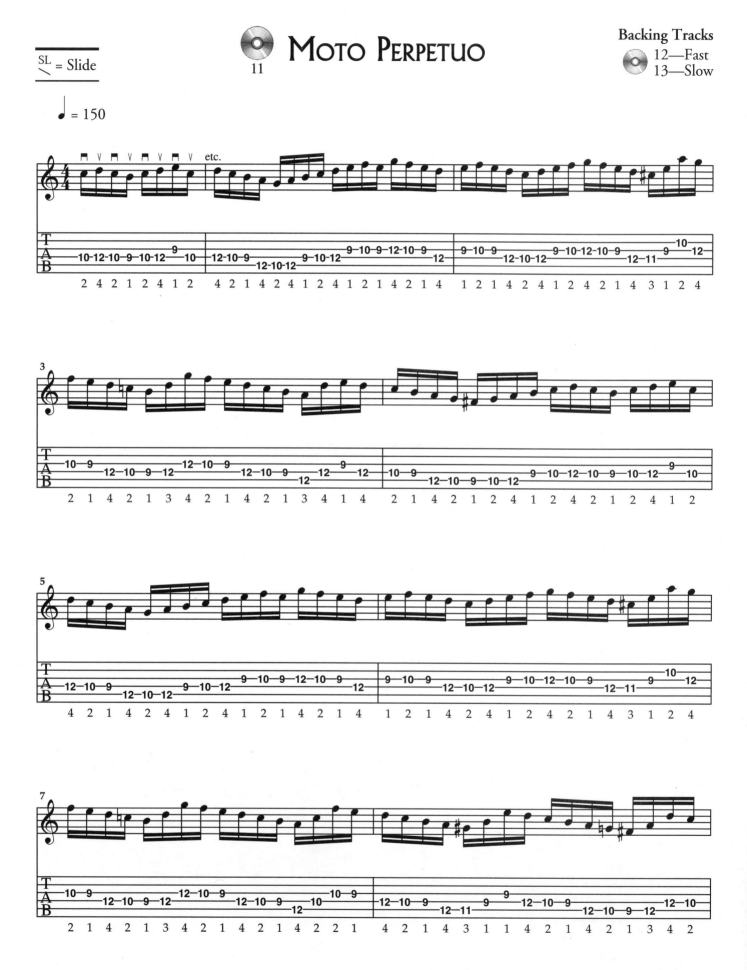

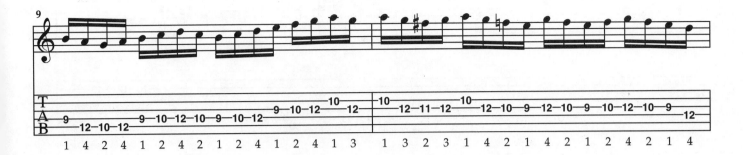

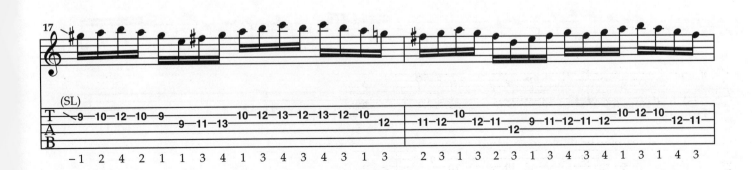

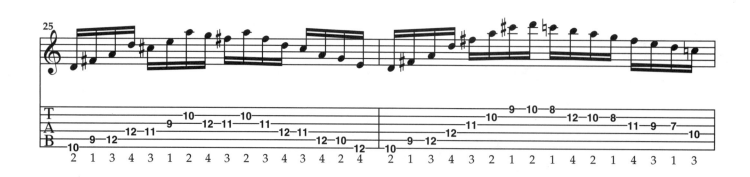

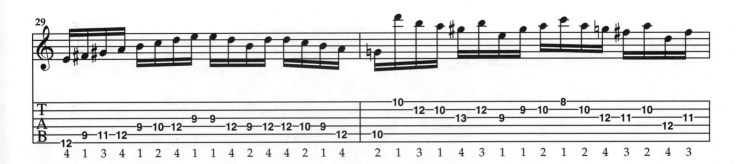

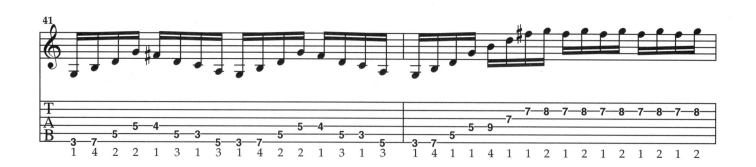

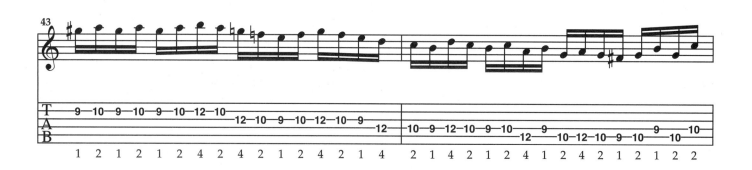

CAPRICE NO. 3

Brief Musical Analysis

Between the years of 1802 and 1817, Paganini composed the collection *24 Caprices for Solo Violin*. The theme of the third piece in this collection, "Caprice No. 3," is an excellent study in octave and legato playing and phrasing. "Caprice No. 3" is in the key of E Minor and in $\frac{4}{4}$ time. The opening theme features octave movement in an ascending i to V (Emin to B) progression. It continues with a similar pattern in the relative major key (G Major), from I to V (G to D).

Measures 1–4

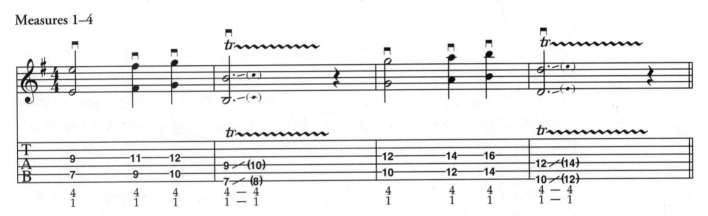

The objective here is to play the theme very cleanly, muting the surrounding strings. The octave shapes of B (in measure 2) and D (in measure 4) are played using trills, which are often used to embellish long, or sustained, notes. On page 12, a trill was defined as a rapid series of hammer-ons and pull-offs between two notes. You can also alternate between the two notes by sliding. Playing an octave trill requires you to slide quickly up and down between the original pitch and the scale step above it.

In Paganini's original composition, all notes are harmonized in octaves. In this arrangement, only the main melodic parts are harmonized in octaves, while the connecting runs are played as single notes. The example below illustrates this combination of octaves and single-note runs. Pay close attention to the phrasing and smoothly connect all of the notes.

Measures 5–6

The implied chord progression in measures 5 through 8 is relatively simple; it connects stepwise from VI (C Major) to v (B Minor) to iv (A Minor) to III (G Major) to V (B7). In measure 7 (beat 4), a non-diatonic A# note implies the secondary dominant (F#7) of B7.

In measures 9–12, the theme is restated one octave higher than in the beginning of the piece.

Measures 9–12

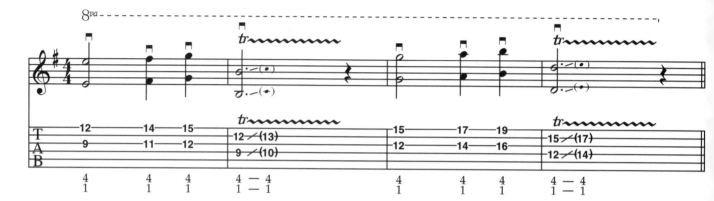

Measures 13–16 feature a development section where the tonal center shifts from the B Dominant sound back to the home key of E Minor. In measures 17–20, Paganini briefly tonicizes the iv chord (A Minor) by playing an A Minor scale, ending on the E Minor chord in measure 20. (Note that the G# on beat 4 of measure 16 serves as a leading tone to A Minor, thus helping to tonicize the iv chord.) The last three measures are based on the chord progression VI–iv–V–i.

Play all the octaves in measures 21–24 with trills, and as previously mentioned, simply slide back and forth from the original octave shape to the shape a scale tone above. The trills on the first beat of measures 22 and 24 are played differently, by just hammering-on and pulling-off only the bottom note (in measure 22) and the top note (in measure 24) and sustaining the other notes played on the open E strings.

Measures 21–24

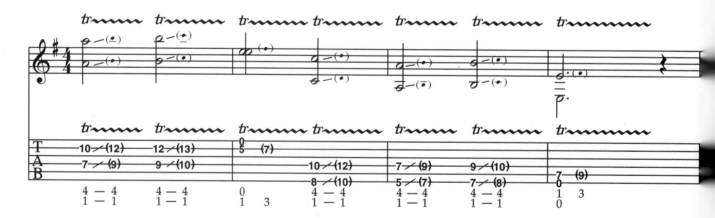

Strive for a smooth and tempered sound. Pick lightly and don't press too hard on the strings when playing legato phrases, as this might cause the strings to go out of tune. "Caprice No. 3" is to be played freely, without a set or steady tempo. Listen to Track 14 on the CD to get a feel for how it is supposed to sound. (Note: the remainder of compositions in this book are arrangements for solo guitar, so there are no backing tracks for them on the CD.)

CAPRICE NO. 3

(Continued on next page)

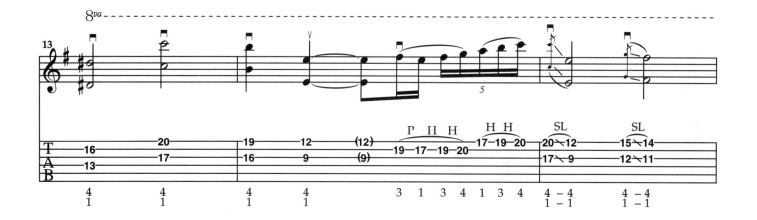

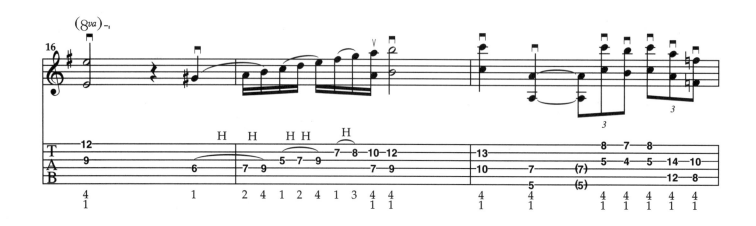

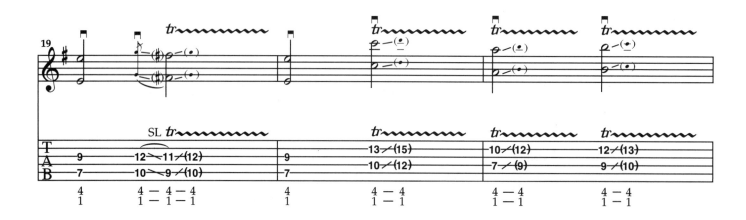

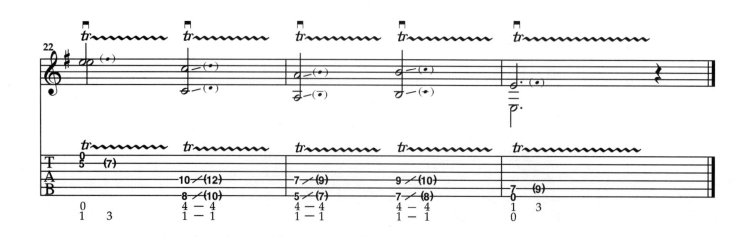

CAPRICE NO. 5

Brief Musical Analysis

The fifth caprice of Paganini's *24 Caprices for Solo Violin* is among the most well-known solo violin pieces of all time. A great performance of this composition can be seen in the famous 1986 movie *Crossroads,* starring Steve Vai and Ralph Macchio.

"Caprice No. 5" begins with a lengthy intro consisting of A Minor arpeggios and A Harmonic Minor scale runs. (The A Harmonic Minor scale consists of the notes A–B–C–D–E–F–G♯, or scale degrees 1–2–♭3–4–5–♭6–7.) The intro—which features rapid arpeggio and scale runs, great for showcasing your chops—is played freely, with no steady tempo. It requires a lot of expression and dramatic execution (for instance, long sustained notes played with good vibrato).

The example below shows an ascending A Minor arpeggio, which is followed by a blindingly fast A Harmonic Minor scale run. This descending line leads back to the beginning of the A Minor arpeggio.

Measure 1

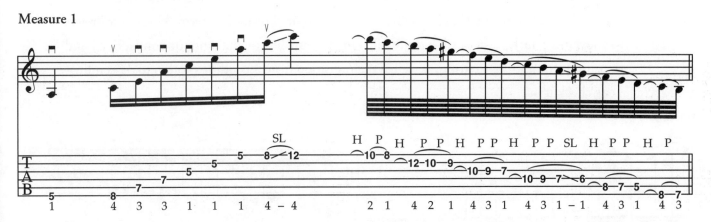

The intro's original arrangement is slightly different from the one in this book, as the range of the violin is greater than that of the guitar. Our version has been arranged to fit perfectly in the guitar's range, while also being comfortable to play.

The arpeggios are all played using sweep picking, and the descending scale runs are performed with a fluid legato style combining pull-offs, slides, and *hammer-ons-from-nowhere* (a technique in which a note is sounded by pressing against the string with a left-hand finger). Each time you go to a new string when playing one of these scale runs, you will use a hammer-on-from-nowhere to sound the first note. It might take some time to master the smooth, clean legato sound, so be patient.

Pay attention to the fingerings for the arpeggios and scale runs, as they provide the easiest combinations for the rapid ascending and descending lines.

In measure 4, there is a tricky tap-bend combination that will require some practice. The *tapping technique* utilizes the fingers of the picking hand to "tap" a note (or notes) against the fretboard at the appropriate fret. (Often, the tapping finger then pulls off to a note already fingered by the left hand, see measure 1 on page 36.) In this case, you tap the 22nd fret of the high-E string with the middle finger of your right hand, bend the tapped note up one whole step (using the right-hand middle finger), and then "release" the bend, bringing it back down to its original pitch.

$\int^1$ = Bend note up one whole step
T = Tap
m = Right-hand middle finger

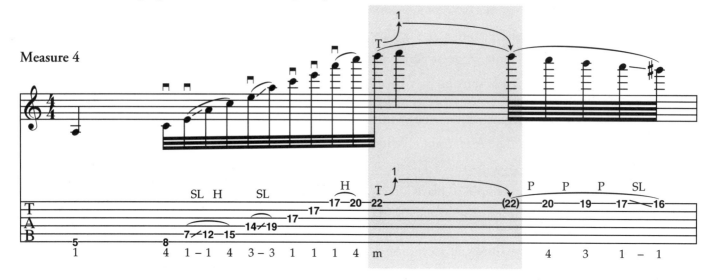

The ending of the intro is a two-octave *chromatic* run—starting on beat 3 of measure 5—that is played with alternate picking and ends in an A Minor chord. (The term "chromatic" refers to movement in half steps.) The difficulty in the run lies in the smooth connections and transitions from string to string, as well as the transition from ascending motion to descending. Let's check it out.

Measures 5–6

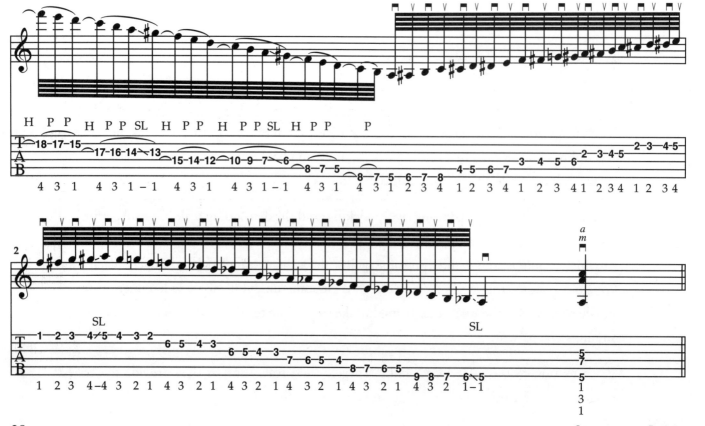

The chromatic run on the previous page is played with four fingers and four notes per string—starting from the 5th fret of the low-E string and cutting diagonally across the fretboard to reach the high-E string. When you get to the end of the ascending line, shift up one fret with your entire hand and start descending the chromatic run to the low-E string. This run is played entirely with strict alternate picking. Due to the four-note-per-string pattern, the picking is simple; you start with a downstroke on the first note of each string, and end with an upstroke on the fourth note of each string.

The main section of "Caprice No. 5" is a rapid sixteenth-note arpeggio and scale etude in A Minor. The theme starts out in the home key and is played entirely with alternate picking.

Measures 7–8

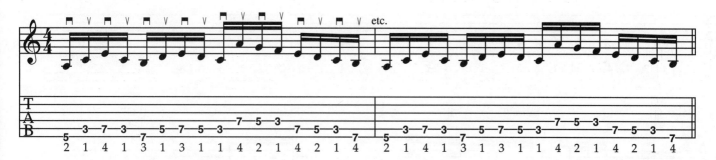

Next is an arpeggio section outlining the chords A, Dmin/A, G7, C/G, and, finally, E7 on the last two beats of measure 4. (Note: A *slash chord* symbol indicates the chord to the left of the slash mark and the bass note to the right. For instance, a C/G is a C chord with a G as its lowest note.)

Measures 9–10

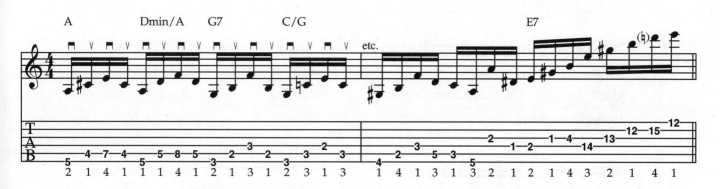

The opening theme is then repeated one octave higher in the 12th position and proceeds to a lengthy arpeggio section, which starts on beat 3 of measure 14 and ends on beat 4 of measure 17. We'll look at this section on the next page.

The progression for this arpeggio section is: C/E, Bdim/D, Amin/C, G/B, F/A, Fmin/A♭, G7, C, Bdim/D, C/E, F, F#dim7, C/G, and G7.

The chords in this arpeggio sequence are voiced in different *inversions* to create a long, descending scale run in the bass. (An inversion is a chord with a note other than the root in the bass.) Check out this section below, and pay close attention to the bass notes as they descend in a line: E, D, C, B, A, A♭, G. The descending bass pattern is then broken as momentum gathers toward the *cadence*, or ending, of the piece.

Measures 14–17

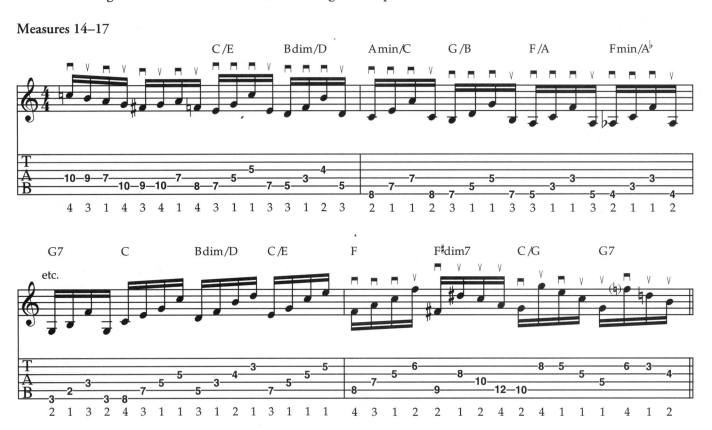

Most of the arpeggios above are played using sweep picking. However, you can also use *hybrid picking*, a technique utilizing the pick as well as the other fingers of your right hand to play and pluck the notes. The short example below illustrates the basic pattern you need to master the arpeggio sequence.

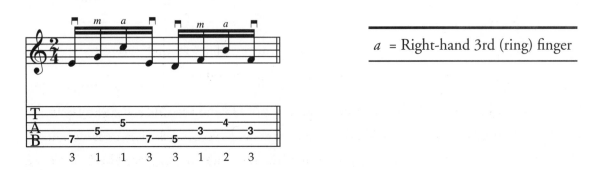

a = Right-hand 3rd (ring) finger

      SHREDDING PAGANINI

The next section is based on scalar *sequences* (repetitions of a musical phrase at different pitch levels) moving through the chords: C, F, D♯dim, Emin, C♯dim, Dmin, G, C, and F♯dim. The difficulty with this passage lies in the mixed use of alternate picking and sweep picking. Pay close attention to the picking directions and practice this section on its own before attempting the entire piece.

Measures 18–20

Immediately following the scale sequence above is a measure with a couple of two-octave arpeggios (C Major and G Major), both of which are played using sweep picking. Be sure to practice the transition from the scalar section to this arpeggio section carefully, as it is very challenging.

Measure 21

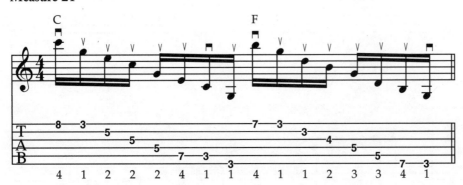

This measure leads into a long chromatic descending run, which is followed by the final alternate-picking scale sequence. The piece ends with an A Minor chord.

Paganini's original arrangement ends with a repeat, then leads into a second ending and extended development section, in which the main theme is restated two octaves higher than originally introduced. I encourage you to study and arrange the remainder of "Caprice No. 5," as it will greatly improve your understanding of Paganini's style and harmonic thinking.

You can hear the solo arrangement of "Caprice No. 5" on Track 15.

Caprice No. 5

⌢ = *Fermata.* Pause, or hold note for longer than its normal value.

Freely

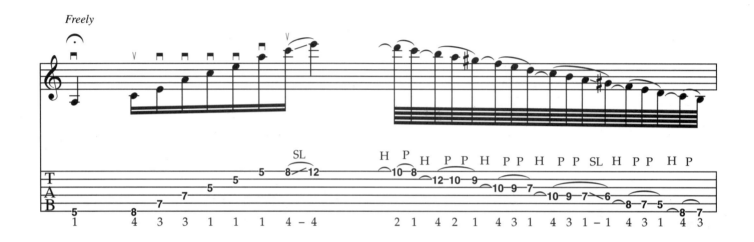

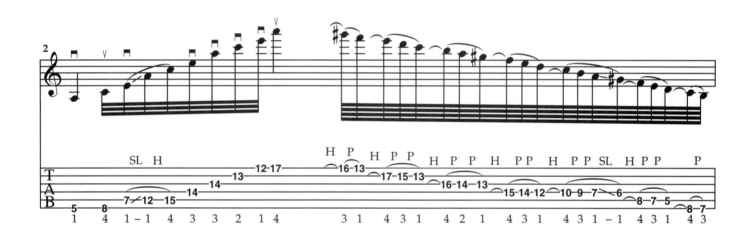

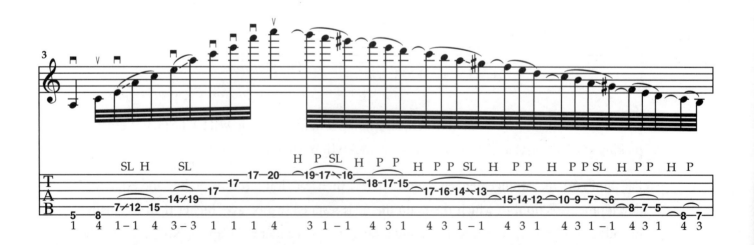

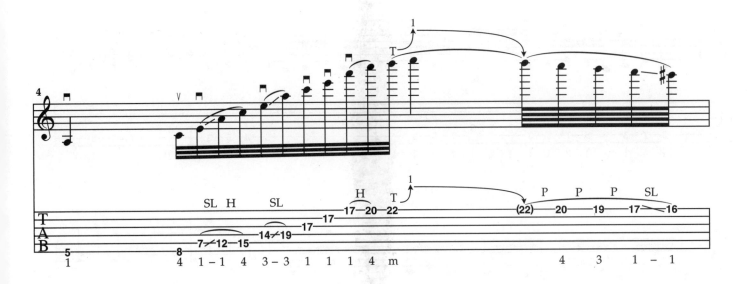

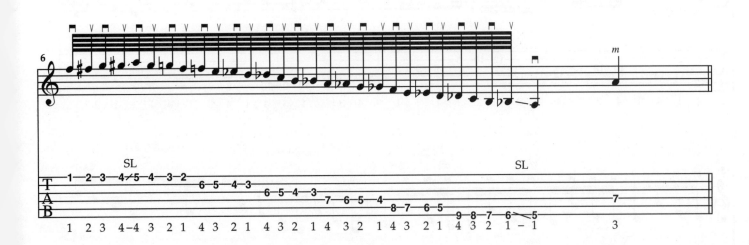

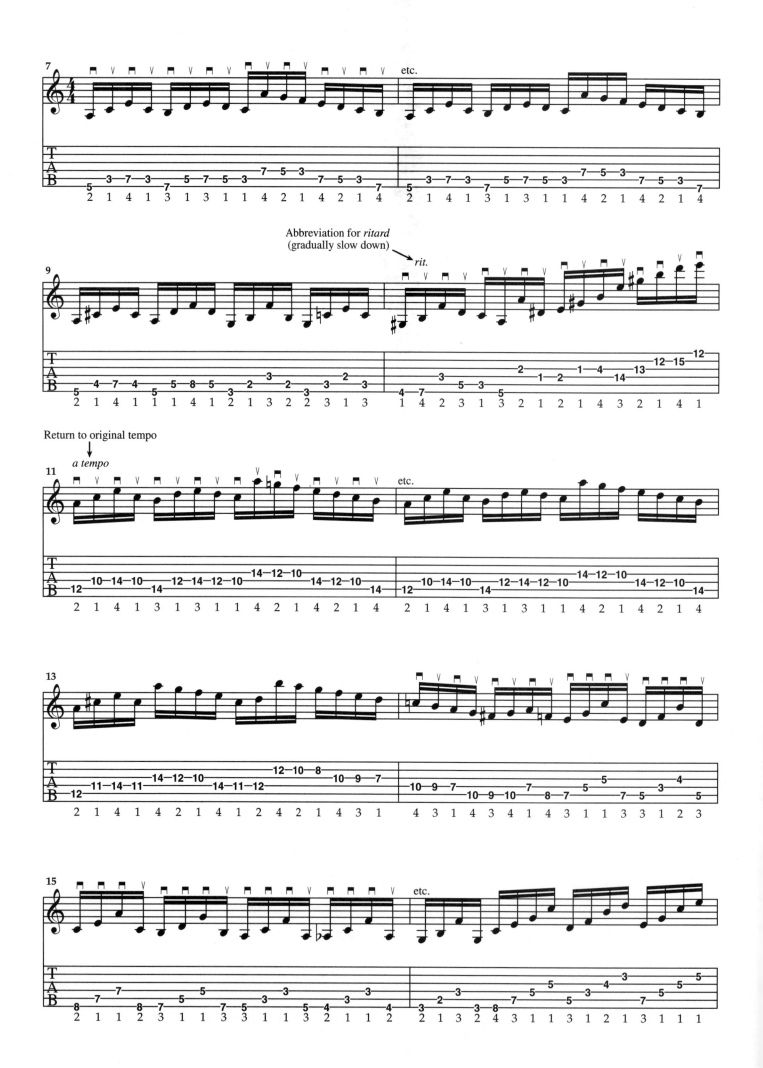

Abbreviation for *ritard*
(gradually slow down)

rit.

Return to original tempo

a tempo

etc.

etc.

etc.

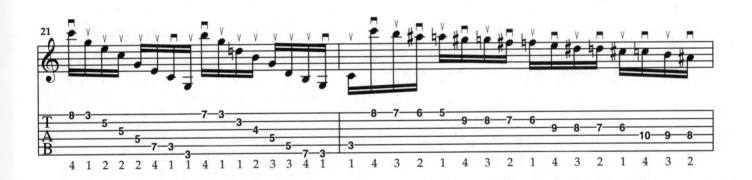

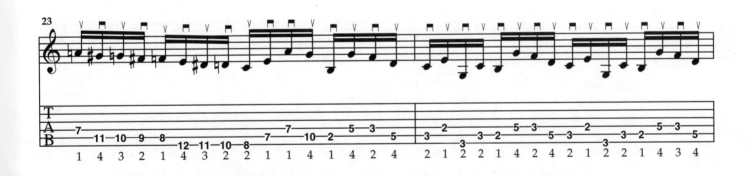

CAPRICE NO. 16

Brief Musical Analysis

Our arrangement of Paganini's "Caprice No. 16" features many techniques, including tapping, alternate picking, sweeping, and hybrid-picking. This piece is in the key of G Minor and is in $\frac{3}{4}$ time. It's played very rapidly and requires a lot of attention to detail, due to the mixture of techniques and range of fretboard coverage.

The basic theme (measures 1–8) starts out with a tapping phrase that outlines a G Minor chord and leads into a *pedal point* and sweep arpeggio of a D7 chord. A pedal point is a note or short musical phrase played against an ascending or descending scale fragment, creating the impression of two simultaneous lines.

Measures 1–2

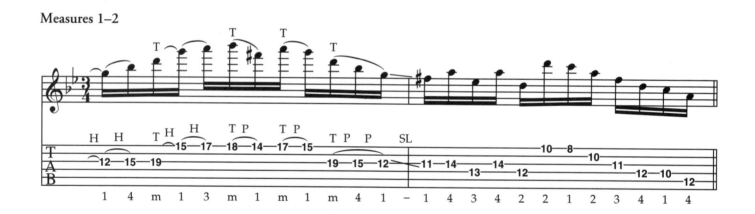

The chord progression for the main theme centers around the i (Gmin) and V (D7) tonalities: Gmin–D7–F♯dim7–Gmin–G7–B♭–Cmin–F7–B♭–D7–Gmin–D7.

The following illustrates the tapping and hammer-ons-from-nowhere used to accommodate the more difficult passages in measures 4–7. As seen in this example, you can also use two fingers of your right hand for tapping. T2 indicates a tap performed with the right-hand ring finger (a). This technique is called *multi-finger tapping*.

T2 = Tap with the right-hand ring finger

Measures 4–6

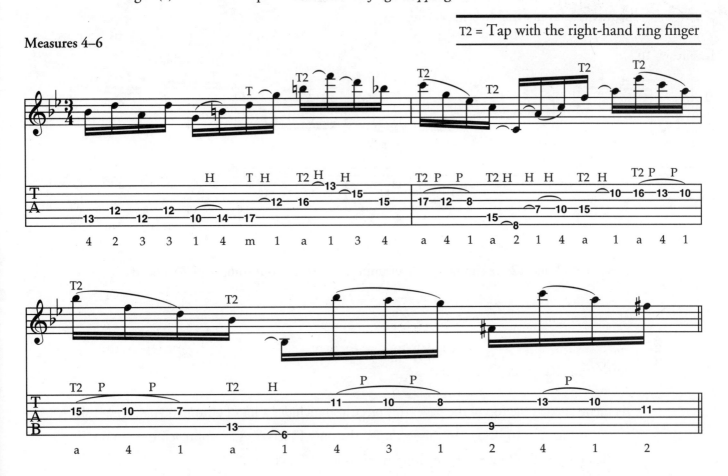

This piece also includes a lot of large interval jumps and pedal points, which can be played using hybrid picking (see page 30). Practice this technique slowly. Make sure to keep the notes from "bleeding" into each other; they should sound smooth, but separate. Also, try to avoid any unnecessary string noise.

Measure 7

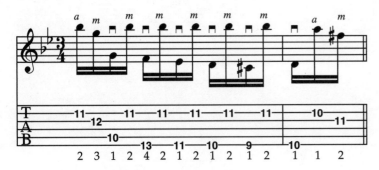

CAPRICE No. 16

The development section features many interesting technical and musical challenges. It includes sweep arpeggios, large interval skips, arpeggio tapping, scale runs, and chromatic runs.

The example below shows a sweep picked G7♭9 arpeggio, which connects to a wide-interval sequence played using hybrid picking.

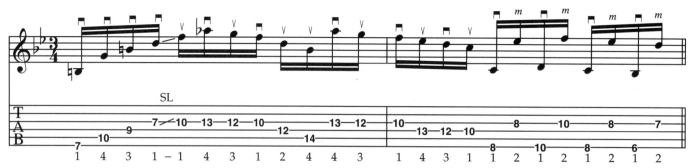

Measures 11 and 12 are similar to the example above, only outlining an F7♭9 chord.

As mentioned at the top of the page, this piece also includes a lot of chromatic passages. Take a look at measure 16 below. In this example, the note F♯ serves as an approach tone to the F♮. Similar chromatic phrases can be found in measures 17–20.

Measure 16

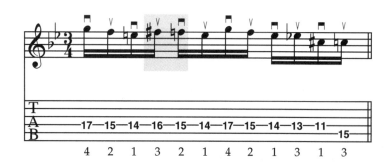

There are also more extended chromatic passages—like the one below—which are usually played with alternate picking or legato. Follow the indicated fingering for easiest playability.

Measure 33

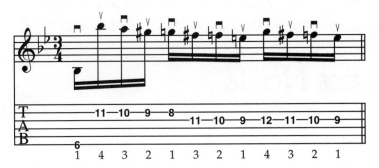

Another interesting challenge is the arpeggio section in measures 27–29. Here, we are using the tapping technique to produce doubled notes, or *unisons*. The first note (and every other note) is played as a hammer-on-from-nowhere, and the following note is played as a tap from the picking hand's index or middle finger.

Measure 27

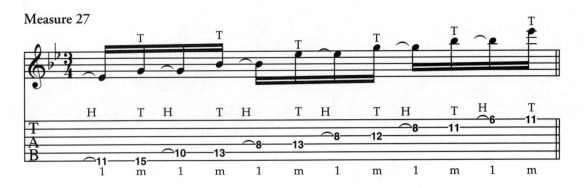

Additionally, the piece contains ascending and descending scale movements in 3rds. This is easiest when played with strict alternate picking. Measure 30 is such an example.

Measure 30

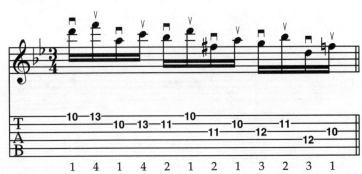

Paganini's "Caprice No. 16" is a relatively long solo piece. It contains many interesting ideas and approaches that will further your technique and understanding of Paganini's compositional style.

You can hear the following arrangement of "Caprice No. 16" on Track 16 of the CD.

CAPRICE NO. 16

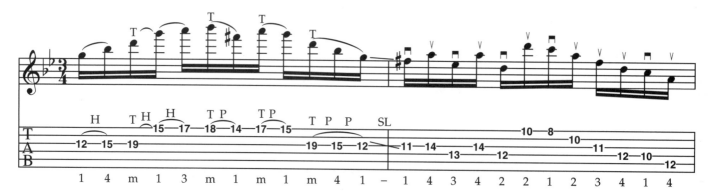

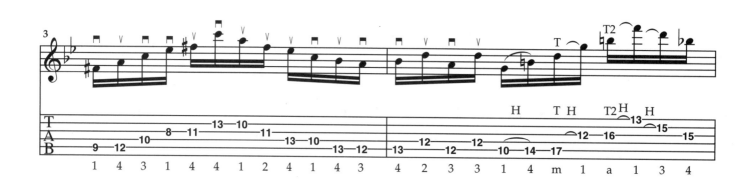

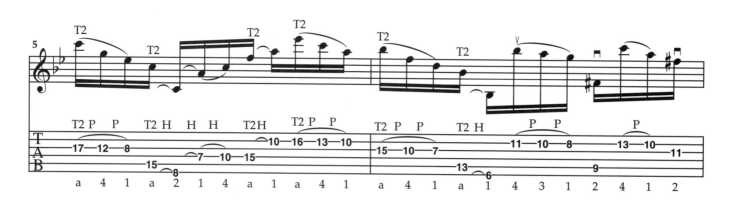

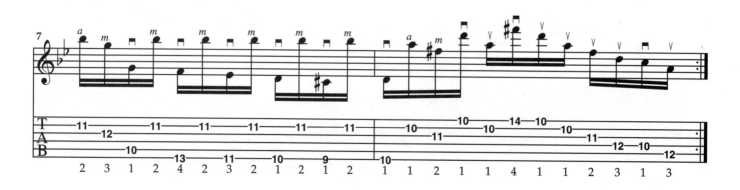

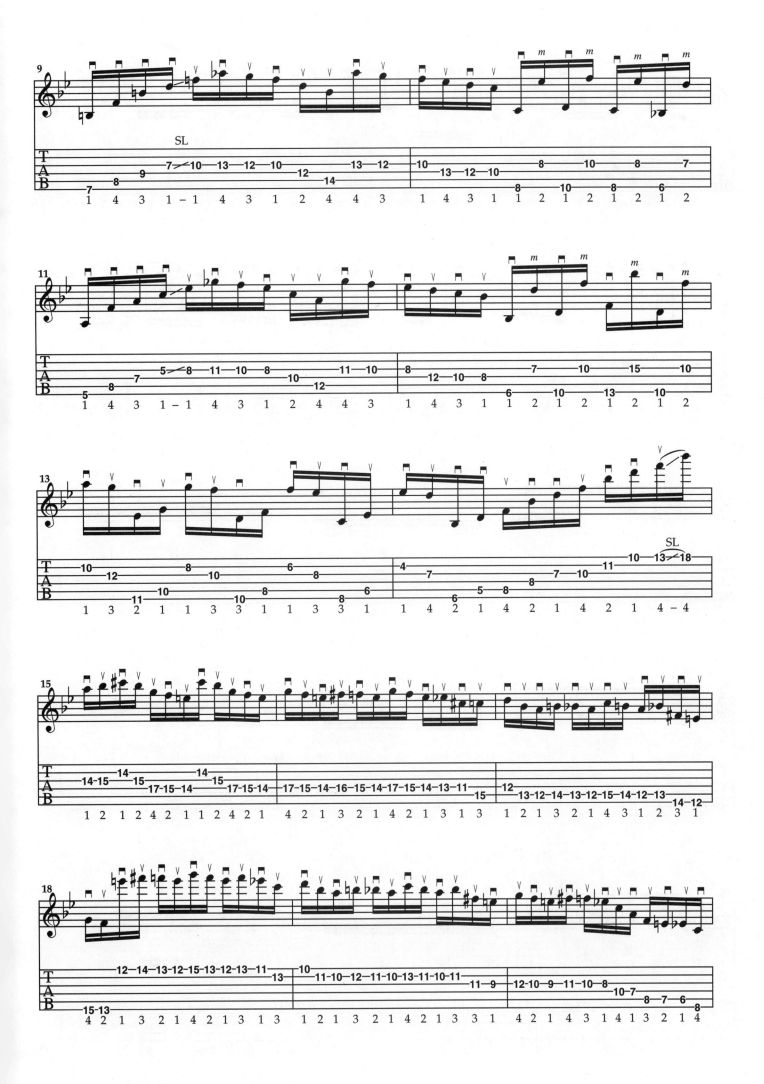

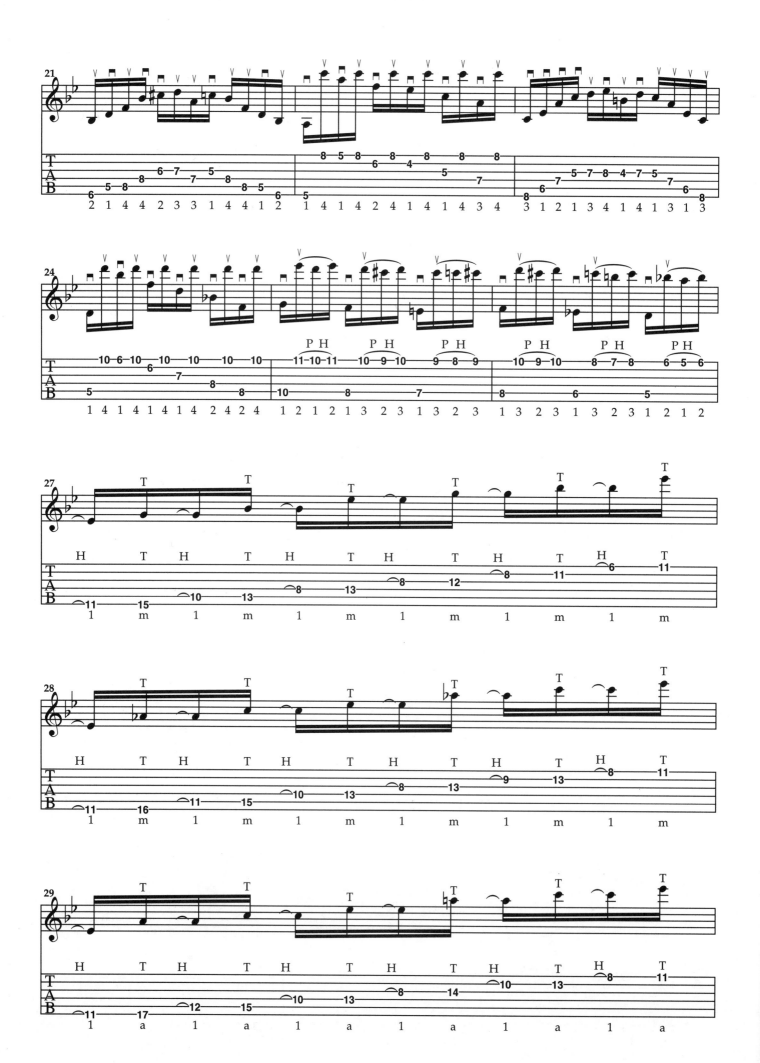

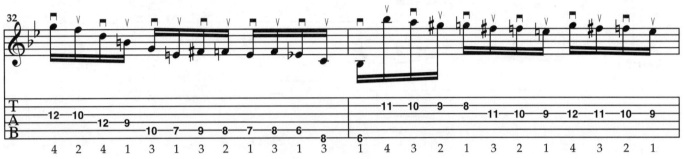

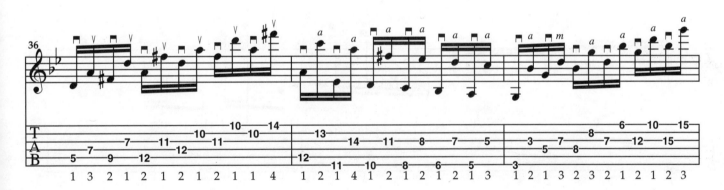

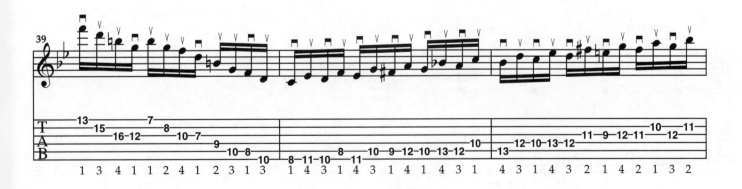

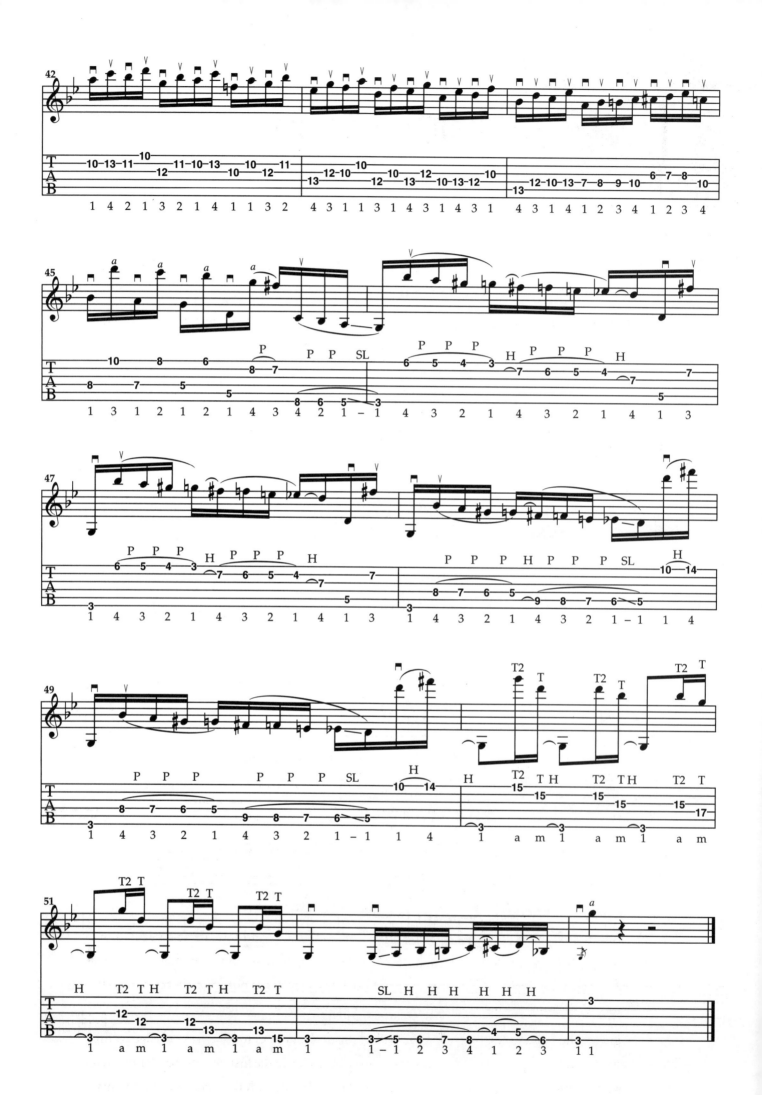

CAPRICE NO. 19

Brief Musical Analysis

"Caprice No. 19" is composed of three different sections. It's in the key of E♭ Major and *modulates* (changes key) to C Minor in the last section.

The caprice begins slow and heavy with a theme in octaves (the notes of which spell an E♭ Major triad) that is then repeated in a lower register. Try to play the octaves slowly and accurately; you can either strum them with a downstroke (muting any unwanted strings) or use hybrid picking to play both notes simultaneously. Connect the notes as smoothly as possible, as this will add a feeling of "weight," or substance, to these phrases.

Measures 1–2

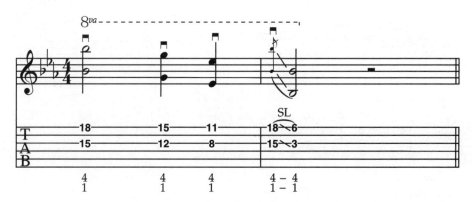

The second section of the caprice, which features an embellished B♭ pedal point, continues with a very light and playful, almost dance-like motif.

Measures 5–6

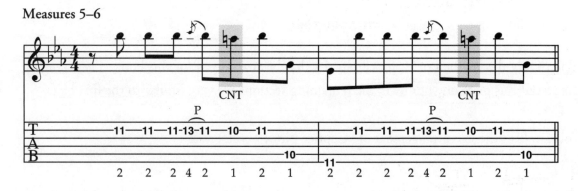

Paganini utilizes grace notes, *chromatic neighboring tones* (CNT), and staccato to give the above phrase lightness and playfulness. (A chromatic neighboring tone is a note one half step above or below another note that returns to the first note.) Try to pick the notes lightly but concisely, and add some palm muting to give the music a staccato feel.

The grace note is performed with a rapid pull-off from the note C to B♭. The challenge in this section lies in smoothly connecting the last note of each measure to the first note of the measure that follows. The motif then moves from the B♭ to an E♭ pedal point, with the same embellishments.

The harmonic implications of this section are relatively simple. The chords are E♭ (two measures), B♭ (two measures), E♭, A♭, E♭, E♭dim/F♯, and B♭.

This is a typical major key progression. It begins on the I chord (E♭), the tonic, and then gradually moves towards the V, or dominant chord, with the help of a secondary dominant or diminished chord that targets the V.

After the repeat, in measures 14–26, the previous motif is picked up again and cycles back through various chords from the V to the I. The last measure of this section, measure 26, is based on a G7 chord and leads to the third section.

The third section of the caprice is in the relative minor key of C Minor. It consists of rapid, scale-based sixteenth-note patterns. Follow the indicated fingerings closely, as this is the best way to master this fast and complicated section. The implied harmony is simple: Cmin, G7, Cmin, G7, D7, G, Cmin, G7, Cmin, G7, and Cmin. Take a look at the first measure of this section.

Measures 27

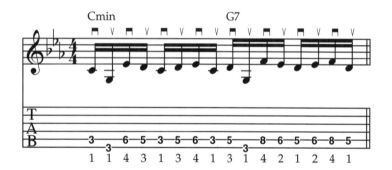

Note: Only the first half of "Caprice No. 19" has been arranged for this book. Try arranging the rest of this piece on your own; the remaining sections are very similar to the first half.

You can hear the solo arrangement of "Caprice No. 19" on Track 17.

CAPRICE NO. 19

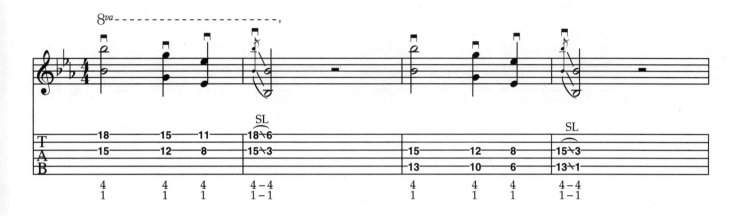

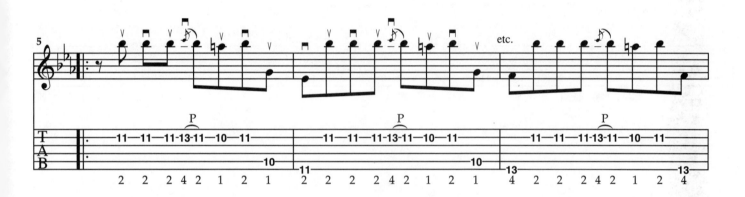

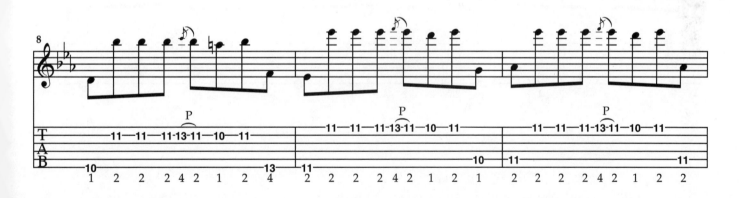

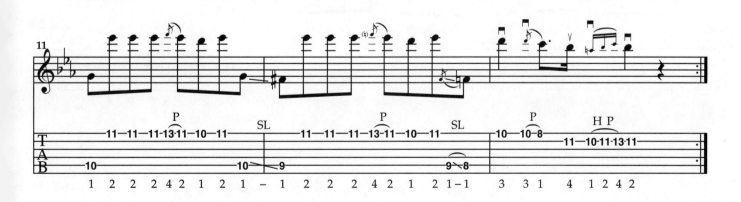

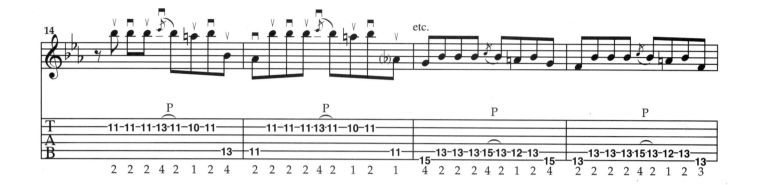

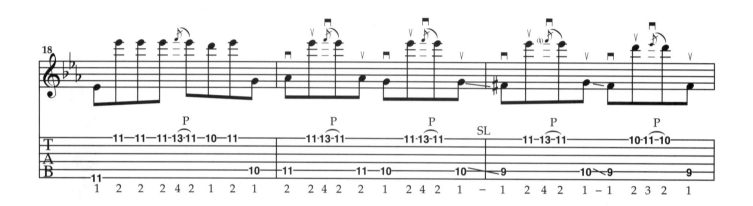

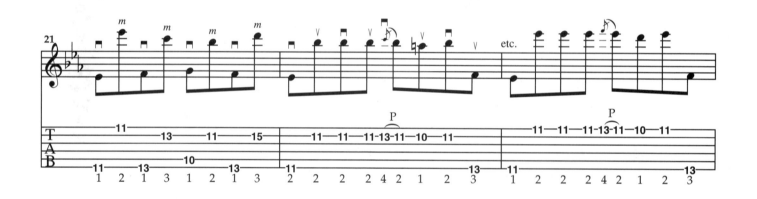

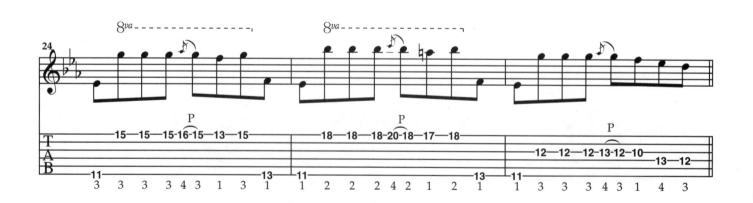

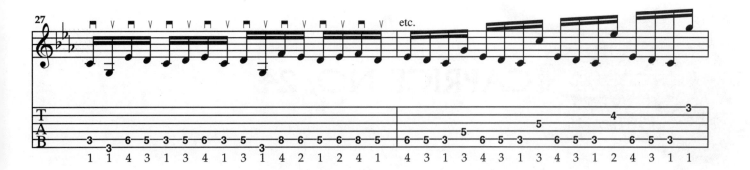

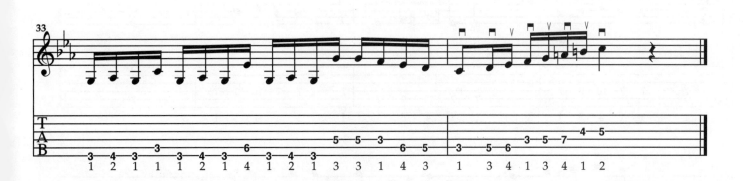

CAPRICE NO. 24

Introduction

Paganini's last piece, "Caprice No. 24," is different from the previous caprices. It consists of a basic theme in A Minor, which is stated and then explored—through the use of different technical ideas—in 11 variations that follow. The caprice closes with a grand finale of cascading arpeggios.

"Theme"—Analysis

Let's take a look at the theme. It is based on the A Minor scale, but also utilizes A Melodic Minor. The melody itself is simple and can be played with alternate picking throughout. The chord progression for the first four measures is: Amin, E, Amin, and E.

The next part, which can be described as the development section, consists of a chord progression based on movement in 5ths. The progression is: A, Dmin, G, C, F, Bdim, F, B7, E, and Amin.

Practice the theme at a fast tempo (around 120–130 bpm). Pay attention to the clean rhythmic execution of the phrases, as this will help give an uplifting feeling to this piece.

🎵 THEME
18

"Variation 1"—Analysis

The first variation on the "Caprice No. 24" theme is based completely on arpeggios and can be played entirely using sweep picking.

Pay close attention to the picking directions, and make sure you play cleanly and accurately.

VARIATION 1

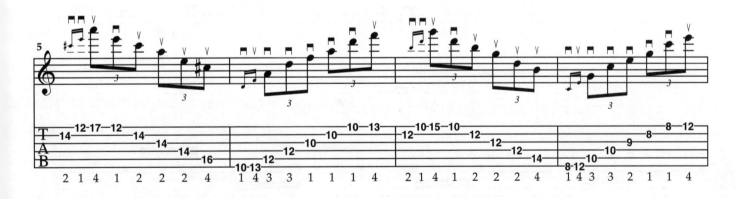

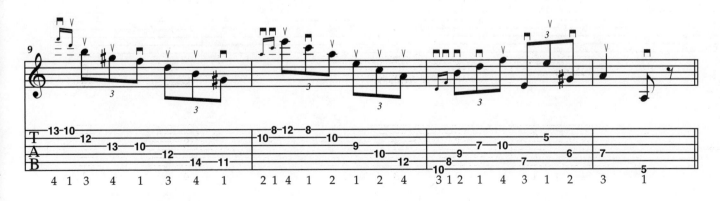

"Variation 2"—Analysis

The second variation is the complete opposite of the previous idea. Based solely on scalar movements and patterns, it should be played with strict alternate picking.

This is a great chops builder; try to practice it with and without heavy string muting.

VARIATION 2

"Variation 3"—Analysis

"Variation 3" takes a different approach to the theme, voicing the melody in octaves. This is a very powerful way to interpret the melody, and the difficulty lies in keeping unwanted strings from ringing out.

Try using hybrid picking to pick and pluck the octaves simultaneously.

VARIATION 3

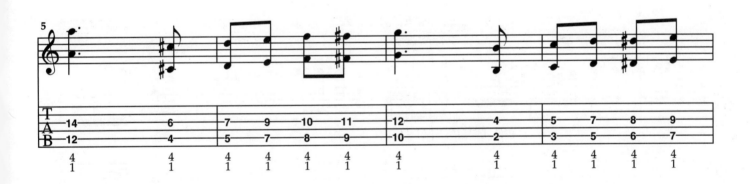

"Variation 4"—Analysis

"Variation 4" utilizes a more chromatic interpretation of the basic theme. It is arranged here using mostly alternate picking but includes some sweep picking as well. You can also use legato techniques for the notes located on a single string, or on adjacent strings. The legato approach will make it sound much smoother and is certainly another great interpretation.

As always, practice slowly at first, paying close attention to correct technical execution and accuracy.

VARIATION 4

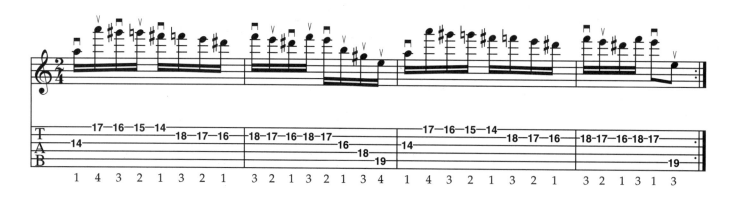

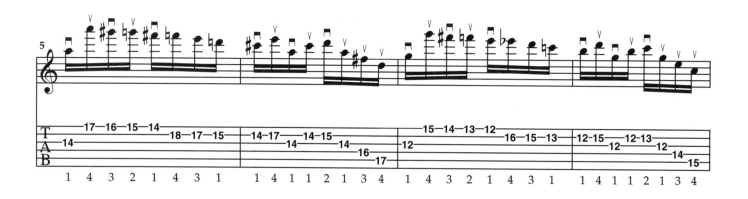

"Variation 5"—Analysis

"Variation 5" uses string skipping and octaves to re-interpret the original idea, almost giving the impression of more than one melodic voice.

Here, the technical challenge of string skipping and octave playing is best met using hybrid picking to cleanly pluck the upper notes and pick the middle and bass notes. Since you will be skipping around quite a bit, it is important to use light palm muting to keep the open strings from ringing.

VARIATION 5

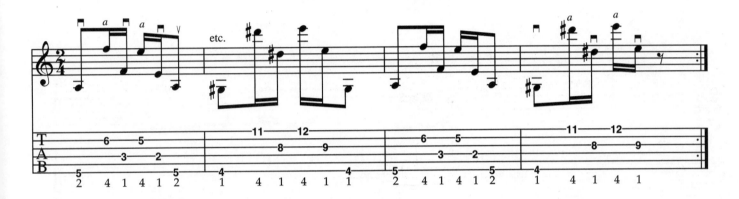

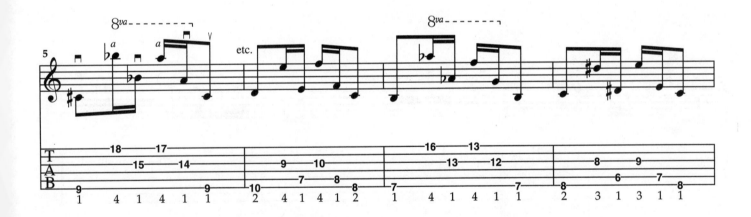

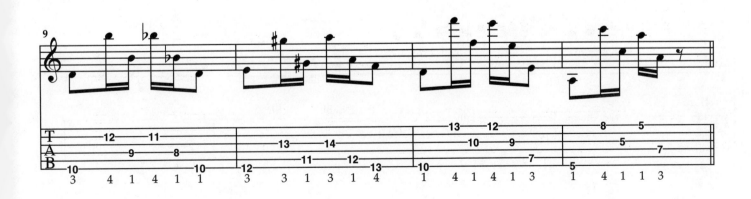

"Variation 6"—Analysis

In Paganini's original version, the melody for "Variation 6" is harmonized in 3rds and 6ths. For this book, however, it is arranged in a single voice to concentrate more on the technical interpretation.

This variation utilizes legato technique, and the objective here is to play the melody as smoothly and coherently as possible. To produce an even and continuous tone, it is important to maintain steady contact with the strings. (In other words, don't remove your fingers from the notes too soon.) As you can see below, very little picking is called for, in order to preserve the smooth legato feel.

VARIATION 6

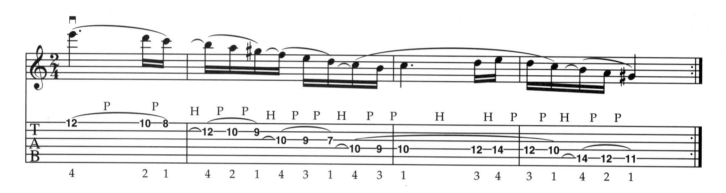

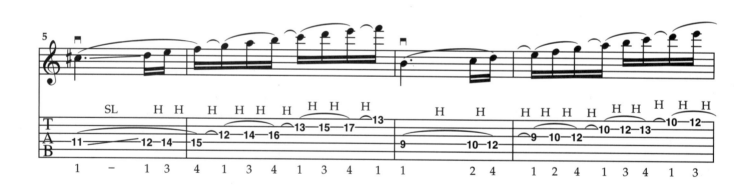

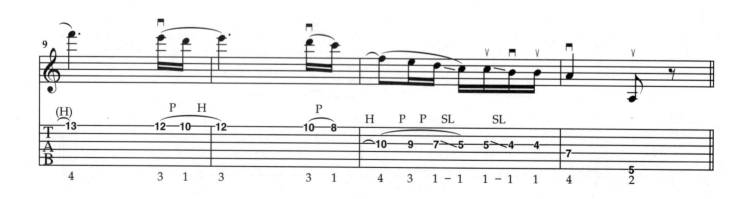

"Variation 7"—Analysis

"Variation 7" is a playful and fun interpretation. It heavily utilizes legato and string skipping techniques, and requires a lot of coordination and string *damping* (lightly muting the strings to stop them from ringing out).

Make sure to accent the first note of each triplet with a pick downstroke, as this will create a strong rhythmic drive.

VARIATION 7

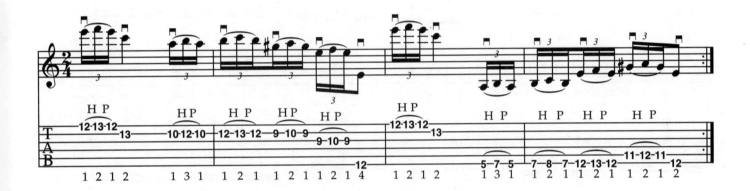

"Variation 8"—Analysis

Paganini's original version of "Variation 8" is based on a chordal arrangement of the theme. For this book, to stay true to the spirit of shredding, the vertical chord structure is arranged as a more linear idea, utilizing the tapping technique to voice the correct notes and intervals.

Try to use a clean, or only lightly overdriven, sound on your amplifier. The tempo is *rubato* (free and flexible), as you need to emphasize the dense note structure and rich harmonies.

VARIATION 8

"Variation 9"—Analysis

The original "Variation 9" was intended to be plucked on the violin rather than bowed (this technique is called *pizzicato*). Pizzicato produces a very precise, but muted, sound. To emulate this effect, this piece has been arranged using a mixture of hammer-ons, pull-offs, picking, and heavy palm muting (P.M.).

To perform this piece accurately requires a lot of coordination, since it combines many different techniques. As always, try to practice slowly, and strive for a consistently muted, but clean, sound.

VARIATION 9

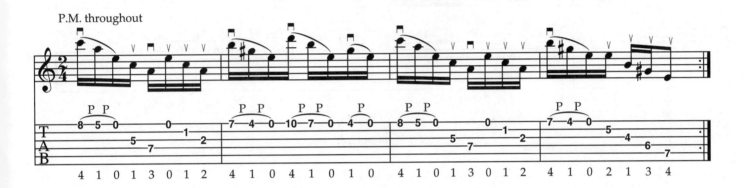

"Variation 10"—Analysis

"Variation 10" offers another great way to perform the original theme in a challenging way. It includes legato, sweep picking, and a wide range of arpeggios.

Again, the performance goal for this variation is a smooth and continuous production of tone, paying close attention to the combination of techniques, while striving for a clean and accurate sound. Watch out for the half-step bend in the last measure.

VARIATION 10

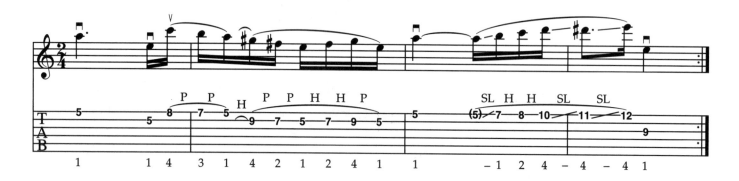

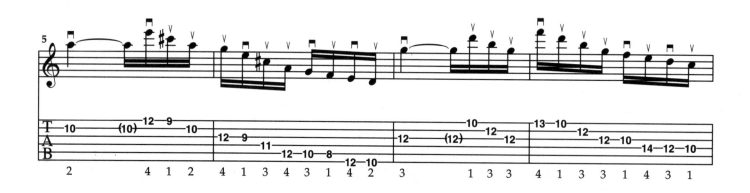

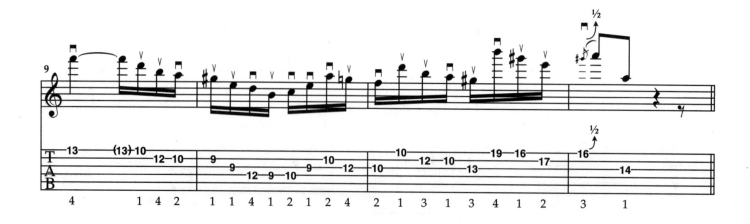

"Variation 11"—Analysis

The grand finale, "Variation 11," is a great showstopper. It includes large intervals skips (played with hybrid picking) and three-octave sweep and tap arpeggios. This variation, which leaves room for your own personal expression and interpretation, should be performed freely.

The chords of Paganini's original arrangement have been reduced to simple intervals that reflect the same harmony but can be shredded.

The first measure is an interval sequence played with hybrid picking. (Make sure to strive for an even sound!) The next measure is an E7 arpeggio played with tapping. This arpeggio requires string skipping, tapping with your 1st or 2nd finger, and a tapped bend from the D to the E on the high-E string (22nd to the 24th fret on the 1st string). The third measure continues with a hybrid-picked interval sequence that leads to an E Major sweep arpeggio in measure 4.

The development section (measures 5–11) draws from the same elements as the rest of the variation. Try to practice these different elements slowly and then combine them.

The last section is a cascading series of A Major arpeggios played with the tapping technique. With each sequence, the arpeggio climbs higher and higher until arriving at the final A Major chord.

Play with the tempo, and other musical devices, to accommodate your own interpretation of this variation.

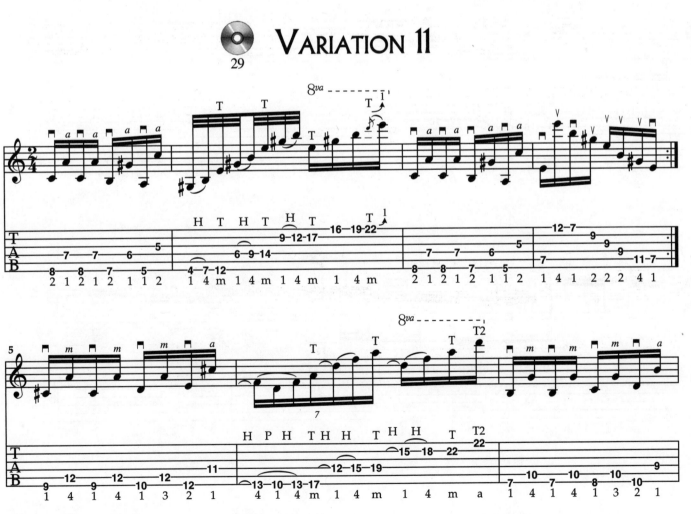

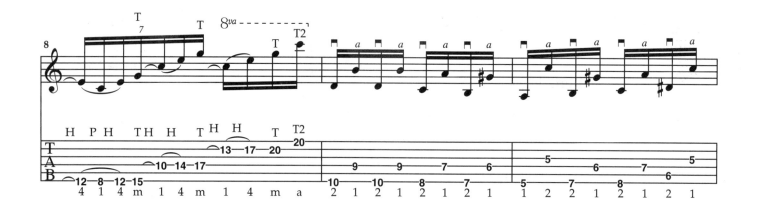

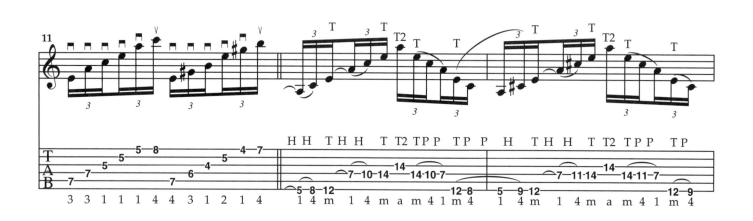

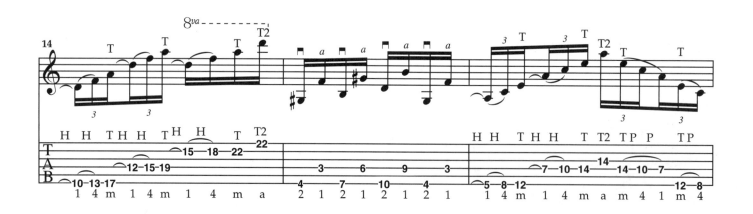

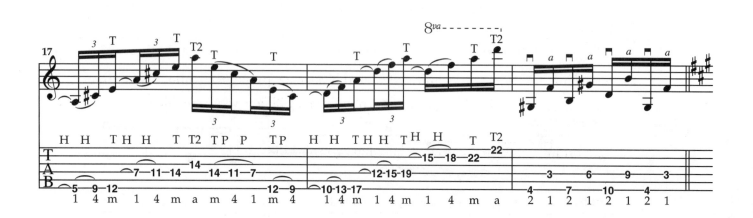

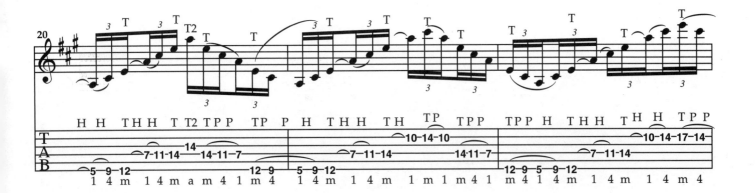

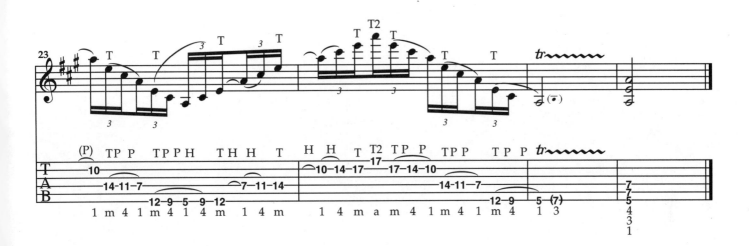

CONCLUSION

Paganini's outstanding work should be viewed in the most positive, inspirational way. He overcame many physical and emotional challenges to become one of the best violinists in history. His example clearly demonstrates what one can achieve, regardless of the obstacles placed in front of us.

When learning the music and technical ideas in this book, be patient and curious. With time and practice, all this will become part of your playing and will flow very naturally.

But the most important thing is to just have fun and enjoy the music.

Shred on!